Pumpkin Stars

Dr. Pao

ISBN: 979-8-88992-386-2

This Book Belongs To:

Dedicated to Christian, And To Pumpkin Lovers
Everywhere

HAVE YOU EVER WISHED UPON A PUMPKIN STAR?

WELL, IT IS NO ORDINARY WISH AT ALL...

YOU SEE, THE PUMPKIN STAR IS ONE IN AN OCTILLION,
SO WHEN YOU SPOT ONE, THERE IS QUITE THE THRILL IN IT

BUT WHEN YOU LOVE PUMPKINS AS MUCH AS ME,
THE PUMPKIN STAR APPEARS QUITE EASILY.

I LOOK UP HIGH AND THERE SHE FLIES, THE MOST BEAUTIFUL PUMPKIN STAR ALIVE!
I CLOSE MY EYES AND COUNT TO FIVE,
I WISH FOR A PUMPKIN WORLD WITH ALL MY MIGHT!

"GOOD MORNING SWEET BOY!" I HEAR MY MAMA SAY,
AS I WAKE UP IN MY PUMPKIN BED.
"WOULD YOU LIKE TO RIDE YOUR PUMPKIN SLED?"
OH YES!   OH YES!   OH YES!

I HOP OUT OF BED AND RUN DOWN THE HALL.
I COULD NOT BELIEVE HOW MANY PUMPKIN PAINTINGS
WERE ON THE WALLS!

THIS WAS MY PUMPKIN WISH. IT CAME TRUE!
I HOPE MY MAMA MADE SOME PUMPKIN SOUP!
I LOOK AROUND AND I CAN'T FROWN FOR
I FINALLY HAVE A PUMPKIN HOUSE! A PUMPKIN COUCH,
A PUMPKIN RUG, I EVEN HAVE A PUMPKIN MUG!

A PUMPKIN HAT,
A PUMPKIN SHIRT,
AND PUMPKIN UNDERPANTS OF COURSE, OF COURSE.

I HAVE PUMPKIN PIE AND PUMPKIN JAM,
I HOPE THERE IS TIME FOR A LITTLE PUMPKIN DANCE.
MY DAD DROVE HOME IN A PUMPKIN TRUCK.
THE WORLD LOOKS SO MUCH
BETTER THIS WAY, I THOUGHT.

I HAVE PUMPKIN MOUNTAINS AND PUMPKIN OCEANS
I WONDER IF THERE ARE PUMPKIN ROSES?
AND PUMPKIN PENGUINS? AND PUMPKIN SHARKS?
OF COURSE, WHY NOT! FOR THIS WAS THE GREATEST PUMPKIN
WISH I COULD HAVE EVER THOUGHT!

AS THE PUMPKIN SUN BEGAN TO SET,
I KNEW IT WAS ALMOST TIME FOR PUMPKIN REST.
I RAN TO MAMA WITH THE BIGGEST SMILE ON MY FACE,
"OH SWEET MOM, TODAY HAS BEEN THE GREATEST DAY."

I HELD HER SO TIGHT AND ASKED IF SHE LIKED HOW I TURNED
THE WORLD INTO A PUMPKIN IN ONLY ONE NIGHT.
"OF COURSE SWEET SON, BUT I'M NOT SURPRISED,
FOR WHEN IT COMES TO FINDING PUMPKIN STARS, YOU HAVE
ALWAYS HAD QUITE THE EYE. I LOVE YOU MY BOY AND DAD
LOVES YOU TOO ITS LIKE PUMPKIN STARS
SHINE THEIR BRIGHTEST, FOR YOU

The End

My First Pumpkin Wish:

My Second Pumpkin Wish:

My Third Pumpkin Wish:

About The Author

Dr. Pao is a children's book author who is dedicated to writing imaginative and magical books for children to enjoy. She draws inspiration from her family and generational favorite, Fred Rogers.